# GRAPHIC BIOGRAPHIES
# MUHAMMAD ALI
## THE LIFE OF A BOXING HERO

*by*
ROB SHONE

*illustrated by*
NICK SPENDER

This edition published in 2009 by Franklin Watts

Franklin Watts
338 Euston Road
London NW1 3BH

Franklin Watts Australia
Level 17/207 Kent Street
Sydney, NSW 2000

A CIP catalogue record for this book is available from the British Library.

ISBN: 978 0 7496 8932 2

Franklin Watts is a division of Hachette Children's Books, an Hachette Uk company.
www.hachette.co.uk

GRAPHIC BIOGRAPHIES: MUHAMMAD ALI produced for Franklin Watts by
David West Children's Books, 7 Princeton Court, 55 Felsham Road, London SW15 1AZ

Copyright © 2006 David West Children's Books

Designed and produced by
David West ⚇ Children's Books

Editor: Dominique Crowley
Photo Research: Victoria Cook

Photo credits:
page 5 (bottom), British Pathe/ITN
page 6/7, British Pather/ITN

Printed in China

**Essex County
Council Libraries**

# CONTENTS

## WHO'S WHO

 **Muhammad Ali** (1942– ) Ali is the only heavyweight boxer to have won the world title on three occasions. He was an anti-Vietnam war activist and, since his boxing career ended, he has worked tirelessly to raise large sums for charity.

 **Angelo Dundee** (1921– ) Dundee used to run Miami's Fifth Street Gym. He trained Ali, as well as other top boxers, throughout his career.

 **Drew 'Bundini' Brown** (1928–1987) As an assistant trainer working with Angelo Dundee, 'Bundini' Brown became a key member of Ali's circle.

 **'Smokin' Joe' Frazier** (1944– ) Frazier was the World Heavyweight Champion from 1967 until 1973. Two of the three fights Frazier had with Ali are among boxing's greatest bouts.

 **Elijah Muhammad** (1897–1975) Elijah Muhammad was the well-known leader of the Nation of Islam (NOI).

 **Malcolm X** (1925–1965) Originally named Malcolm Little, the charismatic deputy of Elijah Muhammad became friends with Ali in 1962. Later, Malcolm X became angry with the NOI and tried to start a rival Muslim organisation.

# BOXING, A SHORT HISTORY

*When Muhammad Ali, fighting as Cassius Clay, won the light heavyweight Olympic gold medal at the Rome Olympics in 1960, boxing had been an Olympic sport for nearly 2,650 years.*

### BRUTAL BEGINNINGS

Boxing was an old sport even before the Greeks accepted it into their ancient Olympic Games. Stone carvings up to 5,000 years old have been found in Iraq, in the Middle East, showing boxers in action.

From Iraq, it spread to the Mediterranean lands, where it became very popular. Men boxed for fun and as a form of military training, though it was very different from the sport we know today. Instead of gloves, the Greeks and Romans wrapped leather strips around their fists. Sometimes, metal studs were attached to the leather to cause injury. Fights were savage, and they were often fought to the death.

### GLOVES ON

*The first boxing gloves were made of leather and padded with horse hair. Modern gloves use foam and other synthetic materials.*

### LOST AND FOUND

Eventually, boxing became too brutal, even for the Romans, and it was banned. As an organised sport it almost disappeared. However, it resurfaced in England in 1661. These early fights were no more than brawls, more wrestling than boxing. Gouging out an opponent's eyes, biting him, and hitting him when he was on the ground were allowed. Men also fought bare-knuckled, meaning without gloves. Many boxers were crippled, and some even died.

Gradually, rules were introduced to ensure boxers' safety. A kneeling man could not be hit, and bouts were given time limits.

## CHANGING TIMES

In 1865, the Marquess of Queensberry supported a set of twelve new boxing rules. The sport was still a vicious spectacle, but the stricter rules meant that it was much safer than before. Bouts were split into three-minute rounds with one-minute rest periods between them. All boxers had to wear gloves and a man would have ten seconds to rise from a knockdown. Also, weight divisions were introduced for the first time, which paired opponents of equal size. Boxing became the sport we recognise today.

## MODERN BOXING

The 1930s, 1940s and 1950s were a golden age for boxing, especially in the United States. Boxers like Jack Dempsey, Joe Louis and Rocky Marciano were household names. However, interest in boxing fell during the 1960s as competition from television emptied the boxing halls. Muhammad Ali changed that. He brought passion, energy and excitement back to boxing, and renewed public awareness of the sport. Boxing became popular again throughout the 1980s and 1990s with champions such as Roberto Duran, Sugar Ray Leonard, Marvin Hagler and Mike Tyson.

ALI IN ENGLAND
*On 18 June, 1963, Ali fought Henry Cooper for the first time. The spectacle was watched by 55,000 people at Wembley football stadium, in London.*

# ALI'S AMERICA

*Proudly wearing his Olympic gold medal, Muhammad Ali entered a restaurant in Louisville, Kentucky, and sat down. Minutes later, he was back outside. Ali had been refused service because of the colour of his skin. The restaurant served only white people.*

## Jim Crow

For Muhammad Ali growing up in Louisville, segregation and discrimination were a way of life. African Americans were separated from white citizens in all public places by rules named the Jim Crow laws, which were named after a black character in a comedy sketch. Facilities provided were of a lower standard than those for their white neighbours. This caused humiliation and offence.

*Rallying Call*
*Martin Luther King Jr* (centre) *pioneered nonviolent protest in the fight for African American rights.*

## Decade of Change

The civil rights movement was jump-started in 1955 by the quiet strength of Rosa Parks. Arrested for refusing to give up her bus seat for a white passenger, her action caused African Americans in Montgomery, in the state of Alabama, to boycott local buses for 381 days.

Parks also helped to inspire the 1963 March on Washington, DC. Three thousand people demonstrated for racial freedom and civil rights for blacks. As the march ended, Dr Martin Luther King Jr, a leader of the march, stood in the shadow of the Lincoln Memorial to deliver his famous 'I have a dream' speech. His vision of a world where everyone would be free hailed the dawn of the modern civil rights movement.

## THE NATION OF ISLAM

The Nation of Islam (NOI) was a religious sect led by Elijah Muhammad, who promoted a version of Islam that stressed African pride, discipline and self-sufficiency. He also preached that the Muslim god, Allah, created Africans and that this made them special. Many white people found these ideas frightening. By 1963, the NOI had over 30,000 members largely due to the efforts of a man called Malcolm X. Elijah Muhammad died in 1975 and was succeeded by his son, Wallace.

*TRAGEDY IN VIETNAM*
*The Vietnam War was the first to be covered by television. Americans were disturbed by the images and many stopped supporting the conflict as a result.*

Malcolm X had become an NOI member while in prison. A charming and persuasive speaker, he was popular within and outside the NOI. It was Malcolm X who first introduced Muhammad Ali to Islam and the Nation of Islam. As time passed, Malcolm X became unhappy within the NOI. He disagreed with some of its teachings and began arguing with Elijah Muhammad. In 1964, on a visit to Mecca in Saudi Arabia, he realised that white people could be good Muslims as well as black people, and, on his return, set up a rival organisation to the NOI that was less strict. On 21 February, 1965, Malcolm X was assassinated by three men linked to the Nation of Islam.

## THE VIETNAM WAR

In the mid-1960s, conflict broke out in Vietnam over the way that the country was ruled. South Vietnam was governed by a democracy, a system where people can choose how to live. North Vietnam was communist, a system where nobody may own anything and everything is shared. America wanted to stop Communism from taking over South Vietnam, in case other countries fell to Communism, too. At first, American soldiers were only involved to advise the leaders of South Vietnam on defence. Soon, the American military was doing all the fighting. Americans had supported the war at the beginning, but this changed. As more Americans died in combat and increasing sums of money were spent, fewer and fewer people believed that the war was worth fighting. Vietnam had divided the nation.

# MUHAMMAD ALI

## THE LIFE OF A BOXING HERO

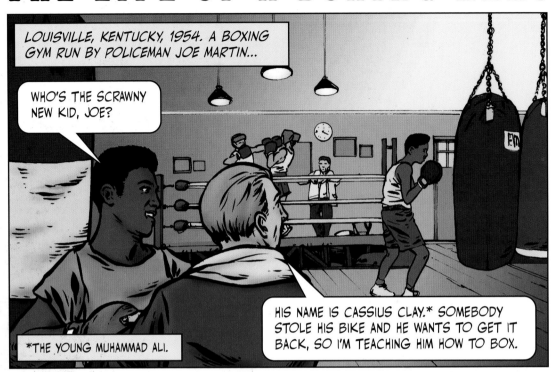

LOUISVILLE, KENTUCKY, 1954. A BOXING GYM RUN BY POLICEMAN JOE MARTIN...

WHO'S THE SCRAWNY NEW KID, JOE?

HIS NAME IS CASSIUS CLAY.* SOMEBODY STOLE HIS BIKE AND HE WANTS TO GET IT BACK, SO I'M TEACHING HIM HOW TO BOX.

*THE YOUNG MUHAMMAD ALI.

IS HE ANY GOOD?

IT'S TOO EARLY TO TELL. IF HE WORKS HARD ENOUGH, HE MAY TURN OUT OKAY.

THE TWELVE-YEAR-OLD CLAY DID MORE THAN JUST 'OKAY'. BY 1959, HE HAD WON ALL THE MAJOR AMATEUR BOXING TITLES IN AMERICA.

AND THE NEW NATIONAL LIGHT HEAVYWEIGHT CHAMPION IS... CASSIUS CLAY!

HOWEVER, THE HIGHLIGHT OF HIS AMATEUR CAREER WAS TO COME.

IN 1960, CLAY WENT TO ROME, ITALY, TO BOX FOR AMERICA IN THE OLYMPIC GAMES.

THERE, THE EIGHTEEN-YEAR-OLD CLAY WON THE LIGHT HEAVYWEIGHT GOLD MEDAL FOR AMERICA.

BACK IN LOUISVILLE, CLAY WAS TREATED LIKE A HERO. THERE TO GREET HIM WERE HIS MOTHER, ODETTE, HIS FATHER, CASSIUS SENIOR, AND HIS BROTHER, RUDOLPH.

ON 24 OCTOBER, 1960, CLAY SIGNED A CONTRACT WITH A GROUP OF LOUISVILLE BUSINESSMEN TO BECOME A PROFESSIONAL BOXER.

THREE DAYS LATER, CLAY HAD HIS FIRST PROFESSIONAL CONTEST. HE WON A SIX-ROUND HEAVYWEIGHT BOUT AGAINST AN EXPERIENCED FIGHTER NAMED TUNNEY HUNSAKER.

I TRIED EVERY TRICK I KNEW TO THROW HIM OFF BALANCE, BUT HE WAS JUST TOO GOOD.

THE LOUISVILLE BUSINESSMEN WERE NOT IMPRESSED.

SURE, A WIN IS A WIN, BUT CLAY LOOKED INEXPERIENCED TONIGHT. WHAT WE NEED IS A PROFESSIONAL TRAINER.

WHAT ABOUT ARCHIE MOORE? HE'S BEEN IN THE GAME LONG ENOUGH.

IN NOVEMBER, CLAY WAS SENT TO ARCHIE MOORE'S TRAINING CAMP IN SAN DIEGO, CALIFORNIA. ONE MONTH LATER...

MR FAVERSHAM? THIS IS ARCHIE MOORE. I'M SORRY, BUT YOU'RE GOING TO HAVE TO TAKE CLAY BACK.

HE TRAINS HARD AND WE'RE ALL CRAZY ABOUT HIM, BUT HE WON'T DO WHAT I TELL HIM TO DO.

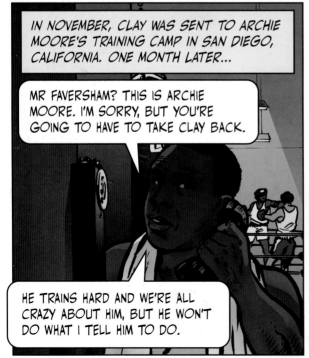

THAT BOY NEEDS TO BE TAUGHT A LESSON, ARCHIE!

HE SURE DOES, BUT I DON'T KNOW WHO'S GOING TO GIVE HIM ONE, INCLUDING ME!

IN DECEMBER 1960, CLAY WAS SENT TO MIAMI, FLORIDA, AND THE FIFTH STREET GYM OF TRAINER ANGELO DUNDEE. HIS METHODS WERE DIFFERENT FROM THOSE OF ARCHIE MOORE.

CASSIUS HAS A STYLE ALL HIS OWN. LOOK AT THOSE FAST HANDS AND FEET, AND THAT NATURAL BALANCE.

BOXERS AREN'T SUPPOSED TO FIGHT WITH THEIR HEADS UP AND THEIR HANDS DOWN, LIKE HE DOES, BUT IT WORKS FOR HIM.

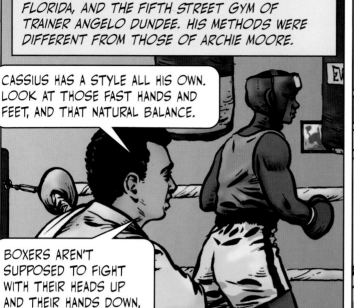

LOOK HOW HE AVOIDS A PUNCH BY ROLLING AWAY FROM IT.

YOU'VE GOT TO UNDERSTAND YOUR FIGHTERS. AND GET TO KNOW THEM.

THAT WAS A LOUSY PUNCH, THOUGH, ANGELO. IT WAS ALL WRONG!

THAT WAS A GREAT RIGHT CROSS, CASSIUS! YOU'RE LEANING INTO IT JUST FINE!

I KNOW, BUT HE'LL GET IT RIGHT NEXT TIME. IF YOU WANT TO TEACH HIM ANYTHING, JUST MAKE HIM THINK HE THOUGHT OF IT FIRST!

THE NEXT TWO YEARS WERE A FRENZY OF ACTIVITY. DUNDEE CHOSE CLAY'S FIGHTS CAREFULLY. HE PICKED EACH OPPONENT TO SHOW CLAY A DIFFERENT BOXING STYLE. GRADUALLY, HE ROSE UP THE BOXING RANKS.

BY THE TIME HE FOUGHT SONNY BANKS, CLAY HAD STARTED TO PREDICT HIS WINNING ROUND. IT ATTRACTED LOTS OF ATTENTION FROM THE PRESS.

SOME OF THE PRESS BOYS DON'T CARE TOO MUCH FOR HIS BRAGGING. THEY'RE CALLING HIM 'THE LOUISVILLE LIP'!

THE MAN MUST FALL IN THE ROUND I CALL. IN FACT, THIS BANKS WILL FALL IN FOUR!

SO WHAT? IT GETS HIM NOTICED. IT HELPS SELL TICKETS...AND NEWSPAPERS!

THE PRESS WERE NOT THE ONLY PEOPLE WHO WANTED TO KNOW CLAY. IN 1961, ON A MIAMI STREET...

EXCUSE ME, AREN'T YOU THAT BOXER, CASSIUS CLAY? MY NAME'S SAM SAXON.

I'VE SEEN YOU FIGHT. YOU'RE GOOD.

I'M BETTER THAN 'GOOD', SAM! I'M THE GREATEST! I'M GOING TO BE WORLD CHAMPION ONE DAY.

LISTEN. THERE ARE SOME PEOPLE I'D LIKE YOU TO MEET. I THINK YOU'LL FIND THEM INTERESTING. HAVE YOU HEARD OF THE NOI?

OVER THE NEXT FEW MONTHS, CLAY ATTENDED NATION OF ISLAM (NOI) MEETINGS. HE HEARD THE NOI LEADER, ELIJAH MUHAMMAD, SPEAK.

WE MUST TAKE WHAT IS OURS BY RIGHT.

HE ALSO MET MALCOLM X.

MALCOLM X MADE A STRONG IMPRESSION ON CLAY. THE TWO MEN BECAME FRIENDS. MEANWHILE, THE WORLD HAD A NEW HEAVYWEIGHT CHAMPION, CHARLES 'SONNY' LISTON.

LISTON STOOD BETWEEN CLAY AND THE WORLD TITLE. CLAY WAS DETERMINED TO FIGHT HIM. THERE WERE A FEW OTHER OPPONENTS TO CHALLENGE FIRST, THOUGH.

ON 18 JUNE, 1963, CLAY FOUGHT BRITAIN'S HENRY COOPER AT WEMBLEY STADIUM, IN LONDON.

CLAY WAS LEADING EASILY WHEN, IN THE FOURTH ROUND...

THE PUNCH ALMOST SENT CLAY THROUGH THE ROPES.

THE END OF THE ROUND CAME JUST IN TIME.

HE DOESN'T KNOW **WHERE** HE IS. I NEED TO BUY SOME TIME. IF I CAN WIDEN THIS TEAR IN THE GLOVE...

REF, A GLOVE HAS SPLIT! WE'LL NEED A NEW PAIR!

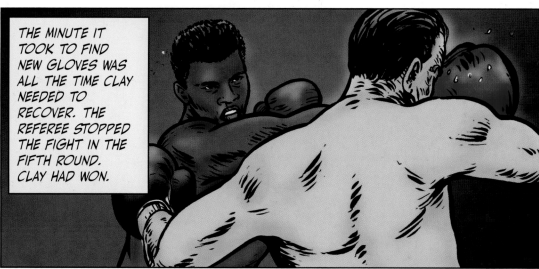

THE MINUTE IT TOOK TO FIND NEW GLOVES WAS ALL THE TIME CLAY NEEDED TO RECOVER. THE REFEREE STOPPED THE FIGHT IN THE FIFTH ROUND. CLAY HAD WON.

LATER, IN THE DRESSING ROOM...

WELL! LOOK WHO'S HERE! JACK NALON!

LISTON'S MANAGER!

HELLO, BOYS. I'VE FLOWN 3000 MILES TO TELL YOU...

...WE'RE READY!

THE LISTON-CLAY FIGHT WAS ON.

TWO MONTHS BEFORE THE FIGHT, CLAY HAD TO TAKE AN ARMY INTELLIGENCE TEST FOR THE MILITARY DRAFT. IF HE PASSED, HE WOULD BE CALLED UP TO SERVE IN THE ARMY AND MAYBE FIGHT IN VIETNAM. HOWEVER, HE FAILED BADLY, SCORING ONLY SIXTEEN PER CENT. THE PRESS WAS SUSPICIOUS.

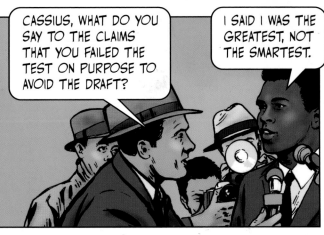

CASSIUS, WHAT DO YOU SAY TO THE CLAIMS THAT YOU FAILED THE TEST ON PURPOSE TO AVOID THE DRAFT?

I SAID I WAS THE GREATEST, NOT THE SMARTEST.

CLAY'S NEW ASSISTANT TRAINER WAS DREW 'BUNDINI' BROWN.

CASSIUS, HOW ARE YOU GOING TO BEAT LISTON? THE PRESS SEEM TO THINK YOU DON'T STAND A CHANCE.

I PLAN TO GET INSIDE HIS HEAD. HE'S GOING TO GET SO MAD AT ME THAT HE'LL FORGET HOW TO BOX! HE'LL BE PUNCHING THIN AIR.

FLOAT LIKE A BUTTERFLY, STING LIKE A BEE, THE HAND CAN'T HIT, WHAT THE EYE CAN'T SEE.

DID YOU JUST MAKE THAT UP, BUNDINI? I MIGHT USE IT MYSELF.

MARCH ON LISTON'S CAMP

WE ALL LOVE CASSIUS CLAY

BEAR HUNTIN'

'lay ENTER

ITHOUT ASSIUS

CLAY NICKNAMED LISTON 'THE UGLY BEAR'. HE THOUGHT UP A NUMBER OF PRANKS AND STUNTS TO ANNOY LISTON.

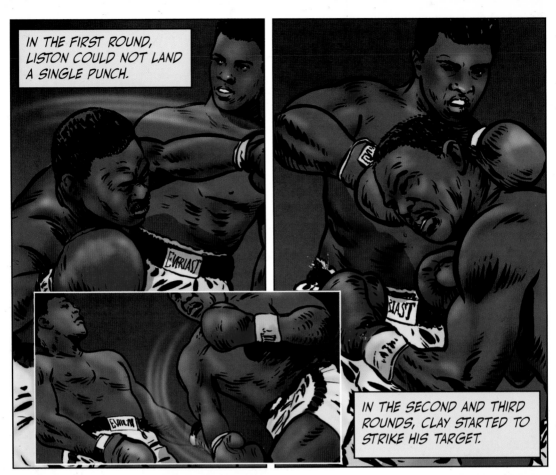

IN THE FIRST ROUND, LISTON COULD NOT LAND A SINGLE PUNCH.

IN THE SECOND AND THIRD ROUNDS, CLAY STARTED TO STRIKE HIS TARGET.

HOWEVER, AT THE END OF THE FOURTH ROUND...

I CAN'T SEE! CUT THE GLOVES OFF! I CAN'T SEE!

HOLD STILL.

I THINK THEY MIGHT HAVE PUT SOMETHING ON LISTON'S GLOVES.

WE'VE NOT COME THIS FAR FOR YOU TO QUIT NOW. GET OUT THERE AND **FIGHT**!

CLAY MANAGED TO KEEP CLEAR OF LISTON'S GLOVES UNTIL HIS EYES CLEARED...

...AND IN THE SIXTH ROUND CLAY TOOK CONTROL.

AT THE START OF THE SEVENTH...

WAIT A MINUTE. SONNY LISTON IS NOT COMING OUT! IT LOOKS LIKE LISTON HAS QUIT! THE NEW HEAVYWEIGHT CHAMPION OF THE WORLD IS CASSIUS CLAY!

I AM THE GREATEST! I AM THE GREATEST! I AM THE KING OF THE WORLD!

THERE HAD BEEN RUMOURS OF CLAY'S LINKS WITH THE NATION OF ISLAM. AT A PRESS CONFERENCE THE FOLLOWING DAY...

CASSIUS, ARE YOU A MEMBER OF THE 'BLACK MUSLIMS', NOW?

I BELIEVE IN ALLAH, THE MUSLIM GOD, AND IN PEACE. 'BLACK MUSLIM' IS A PRESS WORD. THE REAL NAME IS ISLAM.*

*PEOPLE WHO FOLLOW ISLAM ARE CALLED MUSLIMS.

A WEEK LATER, ANOTHER ANNOUNCEMENT WAS MADE. CASSIUS CLAY HAD CHANGED HIS NAME TO THE MUSLIM NAME MUHAMMAD ALI.

WHY WOULD CLAY WANT TO GET MIXED UP WITH THE NATION OF ISLAM?

HE ISN'T A REAL CHAMPION LIKE JOE LOUIS OR FLOYD PATTERSON.

THE LISTON FIGHT CHANGED EVERYTHING FOR ALI. HE HAD A NEW NAME AND A NEW MANAGER, HERBERT MUHAMMAD, ELIJAH'S SON. IN JUNE, ALI MET SONJI ROI. A MONTH LATER, THEY WERE MARRIED.

THE REMATCH WITH LISTON TOOK PLACE ON 25 MAY, 1965. ROUND ONE BEGAN. LESS THAN TWO MINUTES LATER...

GET UP AND FIGHT!

BEFORE THE FIGHT COULD BE RESTARTED, THE TIMEKEEPER CALLED TO THE REFEREE.

STOP THE FIGHT! I COUNTED HIM OUT!

THE PUNCH HAD BEEN SO FAST THAT FEW IN THE CROWD SAW IT. THOSE WHO DID SEE IT THOUGHT IT WAS TOO WEAK TO KNOCK OUT LISTON. THEY SUSPECTED THE FIGHT HAD BEEN FIXED.

BOO!

FIX!

IN JANUARY 1966, THE ARMY LOWERED ITS IQ PASS RATE TO FIFTEEN PER CENT. ALI WAS NOW ELIGIBLE TO SERVE. THE PRESS WAS QUICK TO GET A REACTION.

I REFUSE TO FIGHT AGAINST THE VIETNAMESE.

ALI'S COMMENTS MADE FRONT PAGE NEWS.

HE'S TRYING TO WORM HIS WAY OUT OF DOING HIS MILITARY DUTY.

IT'S UN-AMERICAN.

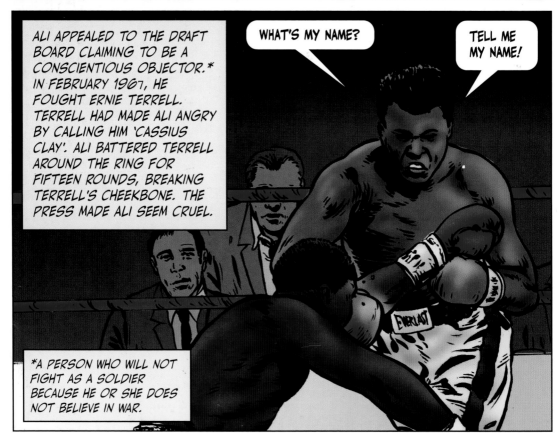

ALI APPEALED TO THE DRAFT BOARD CLAIMING TO BE A CONSCIENTIOUS OBJECTOR.* IN FEBRUARY 1967, HE FOUGHT ERNIE TERRELL. TERRELL HAD MADE ALI ANGRY BY CALLING HIM 'CASSIUS CLAY'. ALI BATTERED TERRELL AROUND THE RING FOR FIFTEEN ROUNDS, BREAKING TERRELL'S CHEEKBONE. THE PRESS MADE ALI SEEM CRUEL.

WHAT'S MY NAME?

TELL ME MY NAME!

*A PERSON WHO WILL NOT FIGHT AS A SOLDIER BECAUSE HE OR SHE DOES NOT BELIEVE IN WAR.

THE FIGHT WITH TERRELL DAMAGED ALI'S CASE AGAINST THE DRAFT. HOW COULD A CONSCIENTIOUS OBJECTOR TREAT A FELLOW BOXER SO VIOLENTLY? THE APPEAL FAILED. ON 28 APRIL, 1967, ALI REFUSED TO BE INDUCTED INTO THE US ARMY.

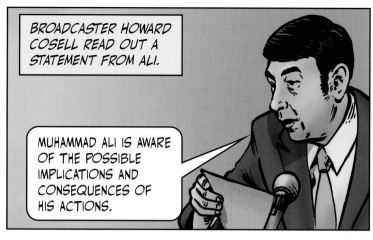

BROADCASTER HOWARD COSELL READ OUT A STATEMENT FROM ALI.

MUHAMMAD ALI IS AWARE OF THE POSSIBLE IMPLICATIONS AND CONSEQUENCES OF HIS ACTIONS.

THE BOXING AUTHORITIES TOOK AWAY ALI'S LICENCE AND HIS TITLE. HE WAS FOUND GUILTY OF EVADING THE DRAFT.

CASSIUS MARCELLUS CLAY, YOU ARE SENTENCED TO THE MAXIMUM TERM OF FIVE YEARS IN A STATE PENITENTIARY AND A FINE OF $10,000.

ALI APPEALED AGAINST THE SENTENCE. THIS KEPT HIM OUT OF JAIL, FOR THE MOMENT.

THEY TOOK AWAY MY LICENCE AND MY TITLE. NOW THEY'VE TAKEN AWAY MY PASSPORT. I CAN'T EVEN BOX ABROAD. HOW AM I GOING TO EARN A LIVING?

ONE OF ALI'S FRIENDS HAD AN IDEA.

WHY DON'T YOU GO ON THE LECTURE CIRCUIT?

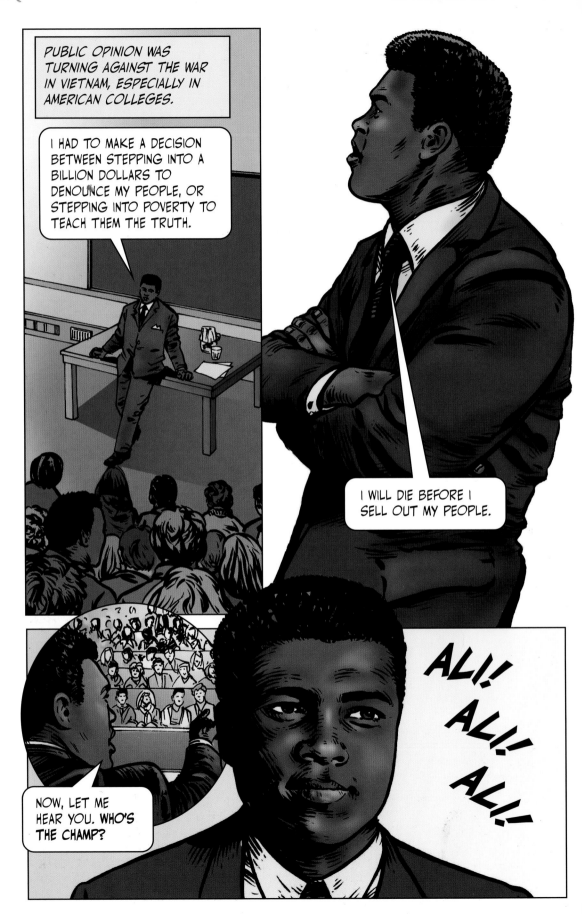

ANTI-WAR PROTESTERS AND CIVIL RIGHTS ACTIVISTS FOLLOWED MUHAMMAD ALI.

PRESSURE WAS MOUNTING ON THE BOXING AUTHORITIES TO LET ALI FIGHT AGAIN. IN THE MEANTIME, HE HAD DIVORCED SONJI AND MARRIED BELINDA BOYD. IN 1968, THEY HAD THE FIRST OF THEIR FOUR CHILDREN, A GIRL THEY CALLED MARYUM.

EARLY IN 1970, THE STATE OF GEORGIA AGREED TO LET ALI FIGHT IN ATLANTA. BY SEPTEMBER, ALI WAS TRAINING IN ANGELO DUNDEE'S GYM.

HE'S BEEN OUT OF THE RING FOR OVER THREE YEARS. I CAN GET HIM IN SHAPE BUT HE'LL BE FACING YOUNGER MEN NOW, BUNDINI.

WHILE ALI HAD BEEN OUT OF THE RING, A NEW FORCE IN BOXING HAD EMERGED. 'SMOKIN' JOE' FRAZIER HAD BEATEN JIMMY ELLIS TO BECOME THE UNDISPUTED CHAMPION OF THE WORLD.

ALI'S FIGHT WITH FRAZIER WAS ARRANGED FOR 8 MARCH, 1971. IT WAS BILLED AS THE FIGHT OF THE CENTURY.

FRAZIER IS SO UGLY HE SHOULD DONATE HIS FACE TO THE BUREAU OF WILDLIFE!

FIGHT NIGHT...

MADISON SQ. GARDEN

IN OTHER BOXERS, ALI'S TAUNTS HAD PROVOKED BLIND FURY. FRAZIER WAS DIFFERENT. ALL HE FELT FOR ALI WAS A COLD HATRED.

CHUMP.

DO YOU THINK YOU CAN BEAT ME?

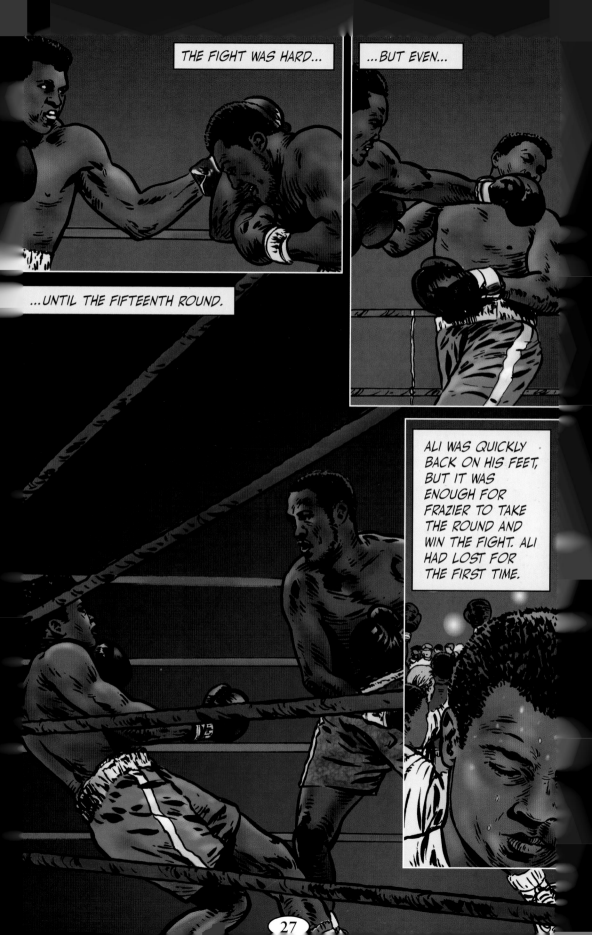

THE FIGHT WAS HARD...

...BUT EVEN...

...UNTIL THE FIFTEENTH ROUND.

ALI WAS QUICKLY BACK ON HIS FEET, BUT IT WAS ENOUGH FOR FRAZIER TO TAKE THE ROUND AND WIN THE FIGHT. ALI HAD LOST FOR THE FIRST TIME.

AFTER THE FIGHT, ALI MET WITH THE PRESS.

SO I LOST. YOU WILL ALL HAVE FORGOTTEN ABOUT IT TOMORROW.

ON 28 JUNE, THE UNITED STATES SUPREME COURT THREW OUT ALI'S CONVICTION FOR EVADING THE DRAFT. ALI SET ABOUT PLANNING HIS COMEBACK.

I WANT MY TITLE BACK, BUNDINI. JOE BEAT ME, BUT HE DIDN'T FINISH ME OFF!

ALI WANTED A REMATCH AS SOON AS POSSIBLE, BUT FRAZIER DID NOT. HE CHOSE TO FIGHT THE HARD-HITTING GEORGE FOREMAN INSTEAD.

ALI, WAKE UP. WE JUST HEARD. FRAZIER LOST. FOREMAN IS THE NEW CHAMP!

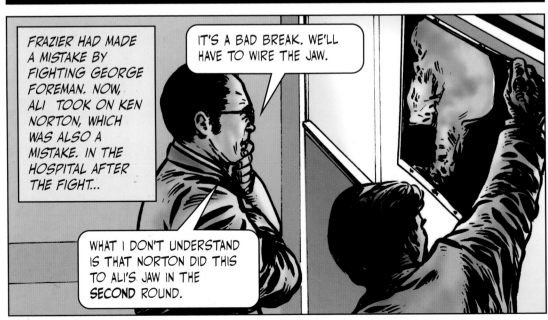

FRAZIER HAD MADE A MISTAKE BY FIGHTING GEORGE FOREMAN. NOW, ALI TOOK ON KEN NORTON, WHICH WAS ALSO A MISTAKE. IN THE HOSPITAL AFTER THE FIGHT...

IT'S A BAD BREAK. WE'LL HAVE TO WIRE THE JAW.

WHAT I DON'T UNDERSTAND IS THAT NORTON DID THIS TO ALI'S JAW IN THE SECOND ROUND.

YET HE FOUGHT ON FOR ANOTHER **TEN** ROUNDS...

...BEFORE HE LOST!

IT WAS A MAJOR SETBACK TO ALI'S PLANS.

IF YOU WANT A SHOT AT FOREMAN, YOU'RE GOING TO HAVE TO BEAT FRAZIER **AND** NORTON FIRST.

SIX MONTHS LATER, ALI BEAT NORTON IN A REMATCH. THREE MONTHS AFTER THAT, ALI FOUGHT FRAZIER AGAIN. ALI HAD LEARNED FROM THE ERRORS HE HAD MADE IN THE FIRST FIGHT...

...AND WON.

WITH NORTON AND FRAZIER BEATEN, ALI BECAME THE NUMBER ONE CONTENDER TO FACE FOREMAN. ALI AND FOREMAN WANTED $5 MILLION EACH FOR THE FIGHT. ONE PROMOTER, DON KING, HAD THOUGHT OF A WAY TO RAISE THE MONEY.

THE PRESIDENTIAL PALACE OF DICTATOR JOSEPH MOBUTU SESE SEKO OF ZAIRE...*

YOU WANT ME TO PAY THE BOXERS $5 MILLION EACH? THAT IS A LOT OF MONEY, MR KING. WHAT DO I GET OUT OF IT?

I WANT THIS TO BE THE BIGGEST FIGHT EVER, MR PRESIDENT! I'M CALLING IT 'THE RUMBLE IN THE JUNGLE'!

*THE CENTRAL AFRICAN STATE OF ZAIRE, LATER RENAMED THE DEMOCRATIC REPUBLIC OF THE CONGO.

ALL THE WORLD'S PRESS WILL BE HERE. IT WOULD BE GREAT PROMOTION FOR ZAIRE.

VERY WELL, MR KING. I WILL PUT UP THE MONEY, AND YOU CAN HAVE YOUR FIGHT.

AND THINK OF ALL THE BUSINESS IT COULD ATTRACT.

THE FIGHT WAS SET FOR 25 SEPTEMBER, 1974. HOWEVER, WITH EIGHT DAYS TO GO, IN THE FOREMAN TRAINING CAMP...

LET ME LOOK AT THAT.

OUCH!

IS IT BAD?

CUTS ARE NEVER GOOD, GEORGE. YOU WON'T BE FIGHTING ON THE 25TH, THAT'S FOR SURE.

THE FIGHT WAS POSTPONED FOR SIX WEEKS WHILE THE CUT HEALED.

WHAT DO YOU MEAN, 'WE HAVE TO STAY HERE'?

MOBUTU THINKS THAT IF WE LEAVE ZAIRE, WE WON'T COME BACK.

WHILE FOREMAN HAD TO WAIT IN HIS HOTEL, ALI TRAINED...

...AND CLOWNED FOR THE PRESS.

RUMBLE ON, YOUNG MAN, RUMBLE ON! FLOAT LIKE A BUTTERFLY, STING LIKE A BEE.

I'M CALLING GEORGE FOREMAN 'THE MUMMY'!

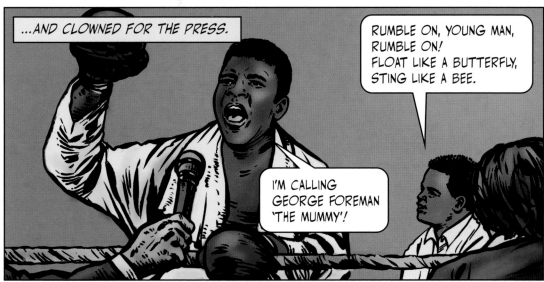

THE WORLD'S PRESS STAYED IN KINSHASA, ZAIRE'S CAPITAL.

WHAT? ARE YOU KIDDING? HE DOESN'T HAVE A CHANCE. FOREMAN WILL WIN! EASILY!

DO YOU THINK ALI CAN WIN?

ALI DID NOT SPEND ALL HIS TIME AT HIS TRAINING CAMP.

KEEP WATCHING THE HANDKERCHIEF.

A QUICK BLOW AND...

...GONE!

SEE ME PUSH IT ALL THE WAY INTO MY FIST.

GASP!

WOW!

HE ALSO ENJOYED MEETING THE PEOPLE OF ZAIRE. HE OFTEN WENT FOR TRAINING RUNS IN THE COUNTRYSIDE.

ALI BOMA YE! AA BOMA YE!

WHAT ARE THEY SHOUTING, BUNDINI?

'ALI, BOMA YE.' IT MEANS 'ALI, KILL HIM.'

'ALI, BOMA YE!' I LIKE THAT!

IN THE ALI DRESSING ROOM BEFORE THE FIGHT, THE MOOD WAS QUIET. THEY ALL THOUGHT ALI WOULD LOSE.

WHAT'S THE MATTER?

THIS IS NOTHING BUT ANOTHER DAY IN THE DRAMATIC LIFE OF MUHAMMAD ALI!

ALI BOMA YE! ALI BOMA YE! ALI BOMA YE!

MUHAMMAD

THE FIGHT BEGAN.

ALI STAYED ON THE ROPES AND LET FOREMAN HIT HIM, ROUND AFTER ROUND.

ALI, MOVE! **MOVE!**

IS THAT ALL YOU'VE GOT, GEORGE?

THEY TOLD ME YOU COULD PUNCH.

AT THE END OF THE EIGHTH ROUND, FOREMAN HAD GROWN TIRED.

NOW, IT'S MY TURN, GEORGE.

A SWIFT COMBINATION ENDED WITH A RIGHT CROSS.

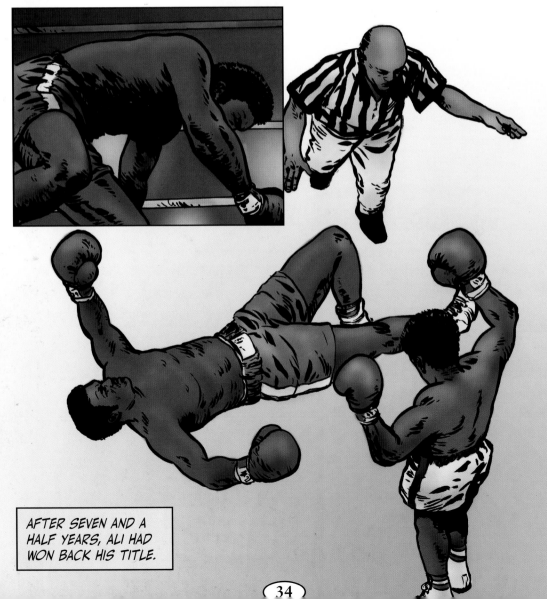

AFTER SEVEN AND A HALF YEARS, ALI HAD WON BACK HIS TITLE.

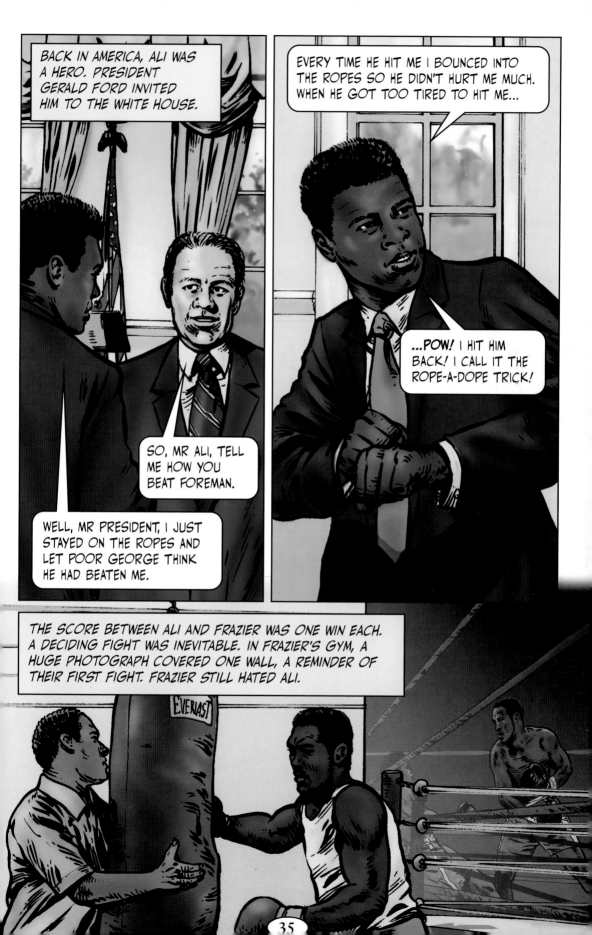

AGAIN, DON KING PROMOTED THE FIGHT. HE APPROACHED THE DICTATOR FERDINAND MARCOS OF THE PHILIPPINES FOR THE PRIZE MONEY.

I WANT IT TO BE THE BIGGEST FIGHT EVER, MR PRESIDENT!

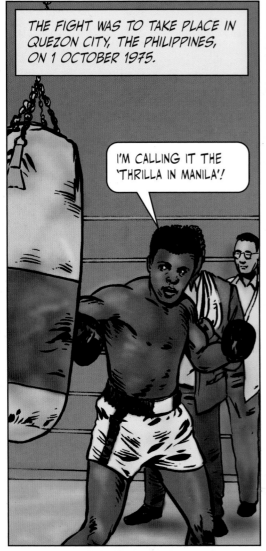

THE FIGHT WAS TO TAKE PLACE IN QUEZON CITY, THE PHILIPPINES, ON 1 OCTOBER 1975.

I'M CALLING IT THE 'THRILLA IN MANILA'!

ALI TAUNTED FRAZIER, WHICH ONLY MADE HIM ANGRIER.

I WANT TO HURT HIM. I WANT HIS HEART!

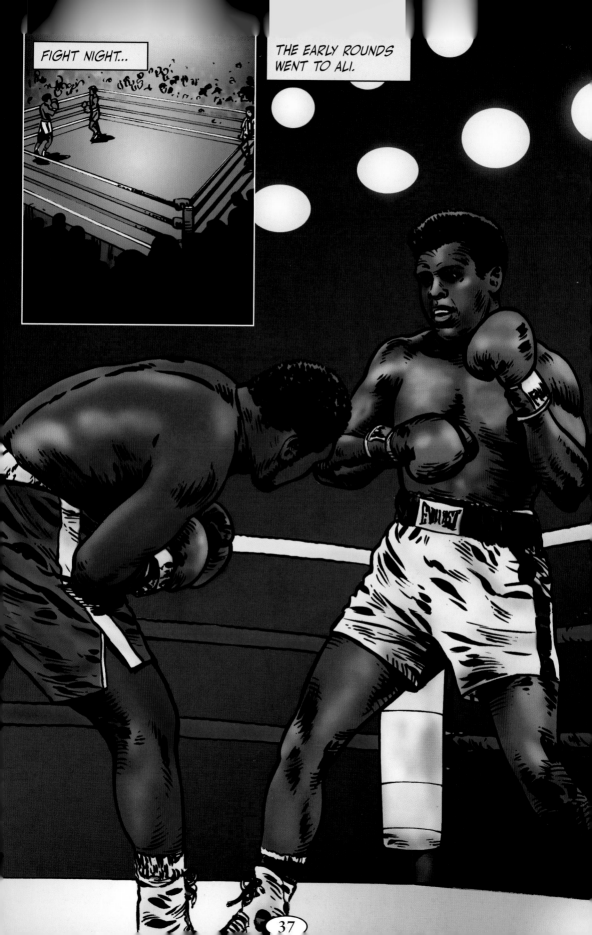

FIGHT NIGHT...

THE EARLY ROUNDS WENT TO ALI.

FRAZIER MANAGED TO CLAW HIS WAY BACK INTO THE FIGHT WITH BODY SHOTS...

...BUT ALI KEPT ON POUNDING FRAZIER'S HEAD.

WITH EACH ROUND, THE FIGHT BECAME MORE AND MORE INTENSE.

IN THE FOURTEENTH ROUND, ALI TOOK CONTROL. ONE OF FRAZIER'S EYES HAD BEEN SWOLLEN SHUT AT THE START OF THE ROUND.

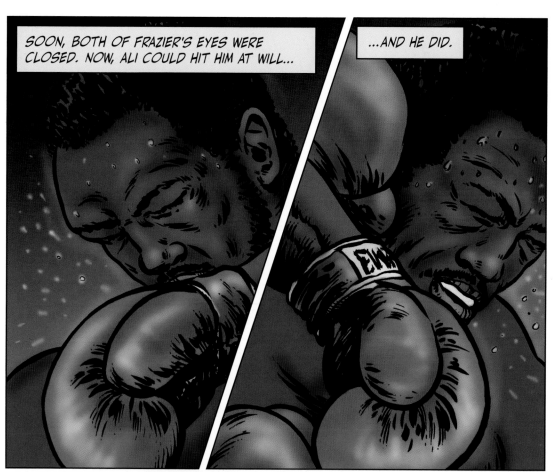

SOON, BOTH OF FRAZIER'S EYES WERE CLOSED. NOW, ALI COULD HIT HIM AT WILL...

...AND HE DID.

AT THE END OF THE ROUND, ALI WAS EXHAUSTED.

ANGELO, LOOK!

IN THE FRAZIER CORNER...

SIT DOWN, SON, IT'S OVER. NO ONE WILL EVER FORGET WHAT YOU DID HERE TODAY.

I HIT HIM WITH SHOTS THAT WOULD HAVE BROUGHT DOWN CITIES.

FRAZIER DID NOT COME OUT FOR THE FINAL ROUND. ALI HAD WON.

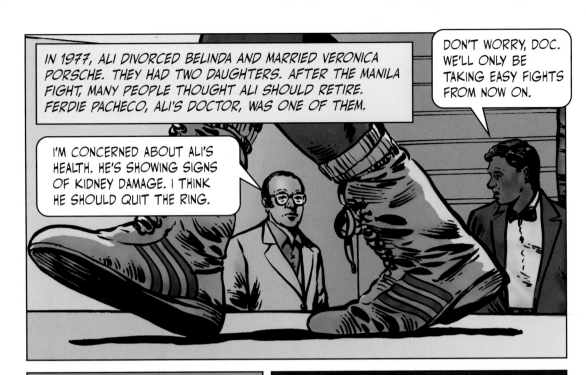

IN 1977, ALI DIVORCED BELINDA AND MARRIED VERONICA PORSCHE. THEY HAD TWO DAUGHTERS. AFTER THE MANILA FIGHT, MANY PEOPLE THOUGHT ALI SHOULD RETIRE. FERDIE PACHECO, ALI'S DOCTOR, WAS ONE OF THEM.

DON'T WORRY, DOC. WE'LL ONLY BE TAKING EASY FIGHTS FROM NOW ON.

I'M CONCERNED ABOUT ALI'S HEALTH. HE'S SHOWING SIGNS OF KIDNEY DAMAGE. I THINK HE SHOULD QUIT THE RING.

ONE OF THE 'EASY FIGHTS' WAS AGAINST A YOUNG BOXER CALLED LEON SPINKS. THE PAIR MET ON 15 FEBRUARY, 1978. ALI HAD NOT TRAINED AS HARD AS HE USUALLY DID.

FOR THE FIRST TIME, ALI LOST HIS TITLE IN THE RING.

IN THE REMATCH, SIX MONTHS LATER, A FITTER ALI BEAT SPINKS EASILY. HE HAD WON THE WORLD HEAVYWEIGHT CHAMPIONSHIP FOR THE THIRD TIME.

AFTER THE FIGHT, ALI ANNOUNCED HIS RETIREMENT.

IN 1980, ALI CAME OUT OF RETIREMENT. HE FOUGHT LARRY HOLMES, THE NEW WORLD CHAMPION. ALI WAS NO MATCH FOR THE YOUNGER MAN. AFTER ELEVEN PUNISHING ROUNDS, ANGELO DUNDEE THREW IN THE TOWEL.

FINALLY, ALI RETIRED FROM THE RING FOR GOOD. HIS HEALTH HAD BEEN GETTING WORSE. IN 1984, HE WAS GIVEN SOME BAD NEWS...

I'M AFRAID NOT, BUT WE CAN TREAT IT.

WHAT YOU HAVE IS PARKINSON'S DISEASE.* THAT'S WHY YOUR SPEECH HAS BECOME SLURRED AND YOUR HAND SHAKES. ALL THAT PUNISHMENT YOU TOOK IN THE RING HAS CAUSED IT.

CAN YOU CURE IT, DOC?

*A DISEASE OF THE NERVOUS SYSTEM.

IN 1986, ALI DIVORCED VERONICA AND MARRIED FOR THE FOURTH TIME. HE MOVED TO BERRIEN SPRINGS, MICHIGAN, WITH HIS NEW WIFE, LONNIE, AND THEIR SON.

IN 1990, IRAQ'S DICTATOR, SADDAM HUSSEIN, INVADED NEIGHBOURING KUWAIT. MANY WESTERN CIVILIANS HAD BECOME TRAPPED AND WERE BEING HELD HOSTAGE. ALI WENT TO THE IRAQI CAPITAL, BAGHDAD...

...AND AFTER TEN DAYS MANAGED TO NEGOTIATE THE RELEASE OF 15 AMERICAN HOSTAGES.

IN 1996, ALI WAS CHOSEN TO LIGHT THE FLAME THAT SIGNALLED THE START OF THE OLYMPIC GAMES IN ATLANTA, GEORGIA.

ON TELEVISION SETS AROUND THE WORLD, THREE BILLION PEOPLE WATCHED THE LIGHTING OF THE OLYMPIC FLAME. MUHAMMAD ALI COULD CLAIM TO BE THE MOST FAMOUS MAN ON EARTH, AND THE 'GREATEST OF ALL TIME'.

THE END

# ALI'S LEGACY

**O**n *15 September, 2000, Kofi Annan, secretary general of the United Nations (UN), made Muhammad Ali a United Nations Messenger of Peace. These are people who have helped to highlight the UN's work.*

## CHARITY

During his boxing career, Muhammad Ali was always generous towards family and friends. Since retiring, he has worked to aid the poor and underprivileged. Ali has helped to deliver more than $50 million worth of food and medical treatment around the world.

*THE UNITED NATIONS Established in 1945, the UN is an international peacekeeping organization.*

### THE MUHAMMAD ALI CENTER

Along with his charity work, Ali has tried to help other Parkinson's sufferers. The Muhammad Ali Parkinson Research Center aims to discover more about the disease and supports those afflicted and their families. What is perhaps Ali's most lasting monument can be found in Kentucky. On 20 November, 2005, the Muhammad Ali Center was officially opened in Louisville. The centre charts Ali's life inside and outside the ring. It also promotes Ali's ideals – global tolerance, respect, understanding and peace.

### YOUNG HOPEFULS

*Like Ali, many young boys started boxing in their neighbourhood rings. For the successful ones, it offered a chance of fame and an escape from poverty.*

# MUHAMMAD ALI'S BOXING CAREER

## Amateur Record
**108 bouts: 100 wins, 8 losses**

## Amateur titles won
1956 Novice title, Louisville, Kentucky
1959 Intercity Golden Gloves Champion
    National AAU Light Heavyweight Champion
1960 Intercity Golden Gloves Champion
    National AAU Light Heavyweight Champion
    Olympic Light Heavyweight Champion

## Professional Record
**61 bouts: 56 wins, 5 losses**

29-10-1960 Tunney Hunsaker W
27-12-1960 Herb Siler W
17-01-1961 Tony Esperti W
07-02-1961 Jimmy (Jim) Robinson W
21-02-1961 Donnie Fleeman W
19-04-1961 Lamar Clark W
26-06-1961 Duke Sabedong W
22-07-1961 Alonzo Johnson W
07-10-1961 Alex Miteff W
29-11-1961 Willi Besmanoff W
10-02-1962 Sonny Banks W
28-02-1962 Don Warner W
23-04-1962 George Logan W
19-05-1962 Billy Daniels W
20-06-1962 Alejandro Lavorante W
15-11-1962 Archie Moore W
24-01-1963 Charley Powell W
13-03-1963 Doug Jones W
18-06-1963 Henry Cooper W
25-02-1964 Sonny Liston W
25-05-1965 Sonny Liston W
22-11-1965 Floyd Patterson W
29-03-1966 George Chuvalo W
21-05-1966 Henry Cooper W
06-08-1966 Brian London W
10-09-1966 Karl Mildenberger W
14-11-1966 Cleveland Williams W
06-02-1967 Ernie Terrell W
22-03-1967 Zora Folley W
26-10-1970 Jerry Quarry W
07-12-1970 Oscar Bonavena W
08-03-1971 Joe Frazier L
26-07-1971 Jimmy Ellis W
17-11-1971 Buster Mathis W
26-12-1971 Jurgen Blin W
01-04-1972 Mac Foster W
01-05-1972 George Chuvalo W
27-06-1972 Jerry Quarry W
19-07-1972 Alvin Lewis W
20-09-1972 Floyd Patterson W
21-11-1972 Bob Foster W
14-02-1973 Joe Bugner W
31-03-1973 Ken Norton L
10-09-1973 Ken Norton W
20-10-1973 Rudi Lubbers W
28-01-1974 Joe Frazier W
30-10-1974 George Foreman W
24-03-1975 Chuck Wepner W
16-05-1975 Ron Lyle W
30-06-1975 Joe Bugner W
01-10-1975 Joe Frazier W
20-02-1976 Jean-Pierre Coopman W
30-04-1976 Jimmy Young W
24-05-1976 Richard Dunn W
28-09-1976 Ken Norton W
16-05-1977 Alfredo Evangelista W
29-09-1977 Earnie Shavers W
15-02-1978 Leon Spinks L
15-09-1978 Leon Spinks W
02-10-1980 Larry Holmes L
11-12-1981 Trevor Berbick L

# GLOSSARY

**amateur** A person who is unpaid for a sport or other activity.

**bout** A boxing match consisting of one or more rounds.

**charismatic** Describes a person, often a leader, who is very convincing.

**conflict** A disagreement between two or more groups of people.

**conscientious objector** A person who refuses to defend his or her country, or attack another country, for either moral or religious reasons.

**dictator** A leader who makes decisions without consulting the people whom he or she rules. His or her actions may or may not be in the people's interest.

**humiliation** When a person is made to feel deeply embarrassed by another's unkind action.

**Islam** A religion based on accepting Allah as God and Muhammad as his prophet. People who follow Islam are called Muslims.

**jab** A short, sharp punch.

**Jim Crow laws** A set of laws in the southern United States that separated white and black people from each other.

**lecture** A detailed talk given on a particular subject.

**licence** A document that grants permission.

**light heavyweight** A boxer who weighs up to 12 stone, 7 pounds as a professional and 12 stone, 10 pounds as an amateur.

**minister** A person who leads a religious ceremony, such as one at a church.

**Parkinson's disease** A disease that is caused by a drop in the production of a chemical called dopamine. It causes shaking hands, slowness of movement and affects balance. It is often associated with old age.

**peacekeeping** Preserving the peace between warring communities.

**penitentiary** US state prison.

**professional** A person who practises a sport or hobby because he or she is paid to.

**protester** A person who makes their objection to something known. He or she may or may not use violence.

**referee** The person who ensures that a bout is fair. He or she may or may not be one of the judges.

**savage** Brutal.

**synthetic** Man-made, as opposed to coming from an animal, plant or mineral source.

**underprivileged** To have fewer advantages than other people.

# FOR MORE INFORMATION

## ORGANIZATIONS

The Muhammad Ali Center
One Riverfront Plaza, Suite 1702
Louisville, KY 40202
Tel: (502) 584-9254
Fax: (502) 584-6009
E-mail: info@alicenter.org.
Web site: http://www.alicenter.org

## FOR FURTHER READING

Ali, Muhammad. *The Soul of a Butterfly*. New York, NY: Bantam Books, 2005.

Christopher, Matt, and Glenn Stout. *Muhammad Ali* (Legends in Sports). New York, NY: Little, Brown, 2005.

Ford, Carin T. *Muhammad Ali: "I Am the Greatest"* (African American Biography Library). Berkeley Heights, NJ: Enslow Publishers, 2006.

Myers, Walter Dean. *Muhammad Ali* (The Greatest). New York, NY: Scholastic, 2001.

Rummel, Jack. *Muhammad Ali* (Black Americans of Achievement). New York, NY: Chelsea House, 1988.

Streissguth, Thomas. *Clay v. United States And How Muhammad Ali Fought the Draft* (Debating Supreme Court Decisions). Berkeley Heights, NJ: Enslow Publishers, 2006.

Ungs, Tim. *Muhammad Ali and Laila Ali* (Famous Families). New York, NY: The Rosen Publishing Group, Inc., 2004.

# INDEX